A Mi1

SAMUEL THAMAR JAMES

Samuel T. James

ISBN: 10: 1537083791
ISBN-13: 978-1537083797

DEDICATION

This collection of poems and spoken words is dedicated to my two brothers, Raymond Jamar Harris and Azania Eleka James..

FIRST AND FOREMOST, I WOULD LIKE TO
THANK THE CREATOR OF THE HEAVENS AND
EARTH, NO MATTER WHAT NAME YOU CALL
HIM BY, RATHER, ALLAH, JEHOVAH, YAHWEH,
THE FATHER, SAME GOD, THAT FASHIONED ME
IN THE WOMB OF MY MOTHER. MY NOURISHER,
MY PASTOR, MY MOTHER, MY MOON, WILLIE
MAE HARRIS, WHO INSTILLED IN ME FROM THE
BEGINNING, THE LOVE OF GOD; MY FATHER,
EMMANEL JAMES WHO TAUGHT ME HOW TO
CARRY MYSELF AND HOW TO DEAL WITH
PEOPLE OUT OF RESPECT; MY SISTERS, ANGELA
MOORE, BRIDGETTE WEBB(MOORE), SANDRA
MAE MOORE, WHO ALWAYS KNOW HOW TO PUT
THE MOST BRIGHTEST SMILE ON MY FACE, AND
THOUGHTS TO THINK ABOUT ON MY MIND; MY
BROTHERS, TRAVIS JAMES, DEMETRIUS JAMES,
RUFUS MOORE JR., AZANIA AND RAYMOND(MAY
GOD BE PLEASED WITH THEM); MY SON, TYREIK
KINSEY(JAMES), MY FUTURE BODY AND SPIRIT,
THAT GOD BLESSED ME WITH TO LIVE LONGER
WHILE THIS FORM IS GONE; MY BROTHERS
FROM ANOTHER MOTHER, SORROD ALI DOGNIA,
OVER TWENTY YEARS IN THE MAKING MY
FRIEND AND COMRADE, AND, VONARD
RUTHERFORD, ALWAYS A SOLDIER I CAN COUNT
ON; MY EDITOR/PUBLISHER, DOMITA WHITE,
LIKE THE SONG SAY, WHERE WOULD WITH OUT
YOU, YOU DID ASPIRE ME TO ACQUIRE; MY
SPIRITUAL FATHER; MINISTER LOUIS
FARRAKHAN, IF I WOULD NOT HAVE HEARD THE
WORD THAT CAME OUT OF HIS MOUTH, THAT

ACKNOWLEDGEMENTS

CONTAINED LIFE, LIGHT, AND POWER, MY MIND
WOULD NOT HAVE BEEN IN TOUCH; MY STEP
FATHER, RICHARD HARRIS, YES, IT WAS ROUGH
DAYS, BUT ALSO GOOD DAYS TOO; MY COUSIN,
TATIANIA POTTER, MY LITTLE RED VELVET
CAKE; MY AUNTY, HAZEL SINGLETON, I THANK
YOU SO MUCH FOR THE MANY LESSONS YOU
TAUGHT ME WHEN I WAS LITTLE BOY, I'LL
NEVER FORGET THOSE LESSONS; AND TO
EVERYONE THAT I DID NOT NAME, BUT STILL
HAD AN AFFECT ON ME, MUCH LOVE TO YOU,
YOU KNOW WHO YOU IS.

DUAL PULL

A desire to go forward, but I just keep getting pulled back.

On the verge of destruction, but the love of life allows me to keep building.

Running from poverty into the hands of riches.

Knowledge pulling, but, ignorance and denial, not wanting to deal with reality, pulls even more.

I want to lose weight, but that chocolate cake is freshly baked.

I said,' I loved her", but I knew my actions pushed her away.

Dark days have me moody; bright days have me in the mood.

It's too noisy, I can't think like that. No noise; and now it seems like something is wrong.

I had love for the life that I had before, but destruction was also attached to that.

So no matter what the up hill road produces, gravity always pursues with it.

PALLIATE

An opiate for a cause not to fix,

Trying to ease the pain, just to stay with.

Searching for a peace of mind, but smuggled by pain, as a hit.

Constantly in the care of an agent, that's not trying to fix.

What's taking me through there to the land of hopeless and despair?

I never knew Palliate was such a teaser.

It knows I love to be teased, even though the desire of getting well, is there to tell.

A mind so robust but busted by snare.

A vision I see so gladly, but looked on by the Lion's stare.

NOT AFRAID TO SPEAK TRUTH TO POWER

Never turn my back to the powers that be.

Never close my eyes to light; not just any light, a light that guides.

I'm out now! Screams not silence to the reality that is.

Courage deeper than the Pacific Ocean.

A gap forming between knowledge and ignorance.

Knowledgeable to your lies; knowledgeable to the truth; and not just any truth; a truth that'll set you free.

Free from the grips of your educational system; your religious institutions, jurisprudence, and more.

Not only do I know, I have to let my brothers and sisters know.

I'm on top of the Mountain with mines.

I don't care if it cost me a check;

I know that what God put in me is worth more than that.

Se'kou Toure' said, "We prefer poverty in freedom to riches in slavery".

Not afraid to say what has to be said.

After all, truth needs a vehicle to ride in.

Why not me? I'll ride to the edge of the sea.

And, even if I have to go in, I'll go in with the mind to win.

And who else would you bring, to go to battle false hood with, other than, Truth!!!

CAN'T WAIT

I can't wait for that day to see the frown on my enemies face.

I can't wait to see the Original Man and Woman back in its rightful state.

That would mean good bye to the bad guys; it definitely wouldn't be a surprise.

They knew their day was coming.

They put up a mean frony.

You know they deserve an Oscar for Well Dressed Truth.

Even though inside, they really couldn't mess with Truth.

I can't wait to take the test of life again.

I know I'll pass it this time.

I've been studying 24 hours a day, 7 days a week.

I better be prepared because life came to compete.

I can't wait to see the Hereafter.

I can't wait to look this judge right back in his face and say,' Here I go!!" like my man Mystikal.

I can't wait to meet Mary J. Blige.

I'm tired of seeing her in a dream, than I wake up, those appearances seems to be the theme of the dream.

I can't wait to laugh in the face of danger.

I can't wait until they open these gates.

I can't wait to hold her in my arms and say," my love, big daddy's home!"

I can't wait, even though I need knowledge and faith, to get me to where I'm going.

I just can't wait.

EUPHORIA

Unfettered by the thought to be; to love and to see.

Non-prejudiced by nature; human nature.

Freedom, Justice and Equality, that produces an ever evolving universe.

Never have to thirst for justice; it comes like the air I breathe.

Never have to I love this; I'm bound by the duty of love to do this.

So elated. Never fooled to go a route I never wanted to choose.

Free will to choose; but with knowledge, wisdom and understanding, not to go the death route.

A passion to overcome, and it's done.

Charting courses, and stepping right through them; high science for the Original Man.

High science for the seed through the vaginal track, when it touches the egg; LIFE!

Such an Euphoric feeling!! A feeling I can't describe in the English language.

But still Euphoria! The joy may you feel when your child

says," I love you dad!"

Yes, that feeling. Nothing holding it back.

Free to pierce any cold heart that was left in the dark.

And even in the dark, an Atom of life sparks; giving new
realities to formalities that is.

So when what I'm feeling takes over with the joy of
victory; dark days and hard times will be left history.

IF YOU ONLY KNEW

If you only knew how it feels to be touched by you.

A touch so electrifying, that it sends a wave of impulses through my body.

You can even just make the mistake of sending me an e-mail, with the letter M, with out sending nothing else and, I'll still know that it meant "miss".

I know, cause I miss you too.

If you only knew that day that I first saw you, you sent my mind into a condition of heaven; right there on the spot.

I always needed to be in a condition heaven.

I didn't know how it really felt, until I met you.

If you only knew. even when you used to get upset with me; the way you frowned your face up, that still was the most beautiful thing I ever seen, something like an oxymoron.

I never thought I will ever put beautiful and frown entwined together.

You're breaking all down the impossibles, like me running a 3 flat, yeah I know it felt like that day you said," You had an emergency, and that your heart was torn and needed me to put it back together.'

A puzzle unbroken by love.

That's what connects our dots.

If you only knew how much I love you.

Yeah, I know you love me too, and I love you, and you may say," I love more!"

And, I'm going to say," Impossible!!'

Even though I know break down all impossibles.

I'm saying, if you only knew. my love held down to the abyss won't even be down there long enough.

It pops right back up; because the force that's directing me to come up out of the abyss is love.

The most powerful force that drives all God's creation. (LOVE)

If you only knew is what I'm saying.

DEATH BEFORE DISHONOR

Before this body be buried and my soul leaves this earth;
it'll be death before dishonor.

What would I take with me and let leave be?

When I'm gone would I leave dishonor amongst my family?

Our God forbids!

Would I let life's struggle crush me under its foot?

Would I let fear over throw me moving forward like the
soldier that I am?

I don't take orders from nobody (except Nature), that's my
wife; we got married twice.

First time I cheated, she took me through there.
Headaches, misfortune and despair.

Second time, I got it right; Heaven, fortune and repair.

Dishonor is a dishonorable thing to me.

It's like going out with the troops and coming back without
the body for its family.

I'd rather you cut off my feet left thrown in the ditch; that's
death before dishonor.

So I honor my ancestors who paved the way for me to be

here today.

I'm talking Marcus Garvey, Elijah Muhammad, Malcolm and Nat.

I'll be dam if I let cowardice spit on their graves!

I didn't forget about you, the lovely Coretta Scott King, Maya Angelo, Harriet Tubman and all my beautiful Nubian Queens.

I know you told the men," It's death before dishonor, I'll breed in our child to win!"

So back to the front line I begin.

Uncorrupted just to pay to win.

Foundation concrete, I serve justice, I don't give a care if it's next to kin; my life has purpose.

An undesirable to lay face down.

Standing on my two feet, just to receive the crown. I'll break the back on these cockroaches who say, Sam isn't focused.

That's death before dishonor, I'll admit, Farrakhan is the one who provoked it.

So, when I'm done breathing that last atom of life, it'll be Death before Dishonor and you can put that there on ice.

A MIND IN TOUCH

In the shadows of the earth, a darkness unreal.

Twenty-four hours back around, a direct light touches the ground.

And what was hidden beneath starts moving.

It starts moving up gradually towards that light.

The light has its undivided attention

A mind in touch signify a once undeveloped mind not in tuned with reality.

In the shadows of the earth represents a false reality not in touch with reality.

The light represents the truth.

It represents knowledge, wisdom and understanding, too.

The ground represents the brain which holds the mind.

The mind hears the truth and starts moving towards that truth.

It has its undivided attention.

A mind in touch with reality. A mind in touch with what is real.

It's like something you can and cannot feel.

It's still real. It's still here. It just hasn't manifested itself yet, through the material.

Touch would have to be connected to material.

The mind guiding it, with the sun striking it.

A mind in touch. I want my mind to grab what it touches.

Hopefully, it touches yours.

But like mines, it was in the shadows of the earth.

I'll give you twenty-four hours with the light beaming off of me.

You would definitely have to come from up under the shade tree.

That same tree got me.

The sun always come back around.

I just decided to take a peek.

Twenty-five years in the shadows of the earth.

A mind not in touch.

I couldn't give you anything.

I didn't have anything to give.

A mind in touch will give your mind exactly what your mind been longing for. Me!!

WHAT HAPPENED?

What happened
to, "hey cuz?" What happened?

Or was it actually, "bye cuz?"

What about "I love you Sam?"

Or was, "I love" covered by deceit?

What happened to the so-called soldiers that said,
"I'll go to war with you", only to give you the words,
"disconnected" from the feet?

What happened?

I was going through the family photo album, it was nice to
reminisce about the love we "had".

Or was it something you just do in the moment as a child
growing up with the figment of the imagination of what
true love is, defined by a world, that goes contrary to what
God is - Love.

Until you get the real world dropped on you, you'll never
know the real true love of someone who says they'll be
right next to you.

I'm talking life, hard times, mixed with the manifestation of
defects.

You'll never know what true love is.

You never know the true you of the true man or woman next to you.

Until the true test comes, the pursuit of (Money, Power, and Respect). Pressure do bust pipes.

But, a little tap, of hard times, no real pressure, just a little tap, drove them far away from me.

What happened?

What about pressure busting up the truth?

They say, "Truth crushed to the ground will sprang back up again."

That's the truth! because I was crushed to ground, and now I've sprung back up again!!

What happened to death before dishonor?

What happened?

What happened to *your* word means everything?

Looks like everything has become your word.

They say, "what happened to you Sam? It looks like you've switch up on us?"

I did. I had too, because my life, being connected to truth, now depends on it.

I definitely didn't want to live a life next to the false you.

I have to stay true to The Truth.

How did you think I've come this far without you?

Surely You'll be the fool for thinking with, I've come this far.

I dam sure didn't pray to you!

Broken homes, ain't nobody getting alone, no pot to piss in, and you want me to come back to that home?!

What happened?

Life happened!

A life free from blood-suckers.

A life free from being trampled under the feet of the ones who say they love you.

Free from always saying what happened to you.

Free from wrestling with the Angel of Death.

So, The Most High, got me so high, above the "what happens", that flying becomes a lethal weapon for protection.

So, looking forward, and not turning back, kept me from

turning into stones, saying "what happened?" to those just happened to perish who've decided to turn back.

What happened?

DIVINE RACE

I'm back in the race for the ultimate prize.

The Hereafter and the meeting with God, have my
undivided attention.

You know how many times I got knocked out of the race?
Let's say 10/29/1984.

I was born thrown into race without proper training.

And what type of runner does not properly train? ME.

I was one of them, or perhaps, billions of them, that either,
jumped in or was thrown in.

But, I'm here now, and I'm not going to stop until that
casket drop.

I'll speak from the grave with my work.

My work will so magnificent and it'll be attached to an idea
that I decided to be apart of when I came into contact with
it.

A superior idea, from everlasting to everlasting.

An idea that was put together by The Creator Himself.

That's the race that I'm running now.

No more 40 yard dashes with the devil.

He was my track coach at first, but I had to switch that up because, life was marathon, not a sprint.

No wonder I was losing all the time.

You can see me now, taking off at the scratch line 10, 20, 30, 40 yards sprinting with my hands raised up, gasping for air like, "I left them fools", until I realized, I was the fool.

So, surely, those who turn back after guidance is manifested to them, the devil embellishes it for them; and lengthens false hopes for them.

That is all the more true. I can't turn back or stop after guidance has been manifested to me.

I'll be a hypocrite, because I bear witnessed to this.

So, I'm running in the race now with the E-lite team. I'll catch you in the Hereafter.

WHY

Why hold on to someone who don't want to hold on to you?

Why hold on to memories that seem like a burden to you?

Why not go to sleep hungry than to wake up in debt?

Why pray for guidance when your intentions are to do wrong?

Why run the race when you're not even prepared for it?

Why settle for less when your Creator has already put it in you to be big?

Why lie?

Why straddle the fence?

Why are you talking so much yet you have so little to say?

Why not listen?

Why buy a chain when you can own the entire field that produces the chain?

Why are we still calling each other Negroes and African Americans?

Why keep saying, "go to school and get a good education",

when we never got anything good out of it but deceit and annihilation?

Why not soar like an eagle?

Why chase after him sister, when he's falling off a cliff?

Why are we afraid to do for ourselves?

Why do we as a people celebrate death?

Why look at the Chinese man with a European name and then say, "that's strange!" He don't even know his own name?" Then he looks at us and says the same thing.

Why do our enemies tell us who our leaders are when we don't even know who are true leaders are?

Why do we keep saying that we're pour when we are the biggest consumers?

Why did my son fall asleep during a test?

They just did a survey and he wasn't falling asleep all by himself.

Why am I asking why?

Because asks why elicits answers.

That's why!

A LOVE TRAMPLED

Up under the feet of suppression.
Suppressed upon the fact, it's a love that can't be given
back.
It was love that had no boundaries and no limits.
It was limitless.
A love aimed at giving itself up to where it was pointed at.
But what it was pointed at, it didn't give love back the
necessary affection.
Wasn't even pointed in love's direction.
It was unaware that love was even there.
So love got trampled on, stepped on like it had doormat
written upon its back.
Love couldn't attack; because the love it had for them was
stronger than a camel's back.
A love still trampled on.
No matter what family, friends and the world could do to
it, it still wouldn't stop love for trying to cherish it.
What was it to cherish?
When what was being cherished didn't give the love back.
Instead, all it gave love was a cold heart and hard stares;
trampled upon the feet, of those who didn't care.
When you love something and someone so much, in the
end of it all, what you loved didn't have that same love; that
same tenacity to give it back what your back was against the
wall.
Sometimes I wonder was I loving out of fear of being left
alone?
How do you define this guiding force?
Even being, trampled to the ground, the the point, when
you still didn't even give it up.

But, you have to remember, a love without no limits or boundaries, when done being trampled upon, the ones it's directed at, you don't give it to that direction again, you point it at a new life, a new wife, a new heaven...etc. You get my drift.

MISCONCEPTION OF REALITY

A misconception of reality have my mind distorted and twisted.

A misconception of what I thought was wrong, ended up being right.

A misconception of my women got me calling her a bitch.

A misconception of reality got me going down the path of degeneracy.

My mind being bogged down with the weight of false reality.

My mind being bogged down with the weight of thinking I'm my own man.

Still sinking in the quick sand of thinking, I'm my own man; while deep down inside, only wishing, there was somebody there to grab "my own man" hand.

Misconception of reality, and self, got me praying to a mystery god for help.

Not knowing that God is closer to me than my jugular vein.

Insane, right? (Not insane!), if misconception stood between me and how I perceived reality.

But how would I know if I perceived reality in the right way?

How would I know, except I have a teacher, and how would I have a teacher, unless he be sent?

Misconception of reality got me pointing my weapon (mind) in the wrong direction.

Misconception rooted in the seed of ignorance, and cultivated by memory of forgetfulness, got me blind to realness.

Misconception of Reality is no reality at all.

And if that is the case, why when Truth comes on the scene, misconception of what I perceived as wrong, was the only thing standing.
Where did all the misconception go at?
It never existed!!
It was all a condition of the mind, and when my mind changed, reality came with it.

SILHOUETTE CHASING

I knows what you represent, an outline that my eyes see
that my senses can't connect with.

The unseen reality is overlapped by your silhouette.

I'm steady chasing what arouses the nature, my destination
never quite there yet.

An outline has its limit.

But what expresses itself, is unlimited by how it expresses
itself, through the limit.

A mind un-timid, a rhyme not finished, my thought
connected to this pen is just the beginning.

Your aroma, latched to my nostrils, put me on the hunt,
even though I know it might not go well.

Deaf ears hoping it can hear, so it tells itself," Hey, who
goes there?"

The walls talking, dogs barking, those alarmist keep me up
on post.

I had a vision, darkly tented, I thought you pulled up in a
ghost.

Grab the flashlight, wanting to flash light, but the road to
your heart was just that tight.

Chasing silhouette, while silhouette chasing, I had to tell myself, be patient,

I'll be here up all night.

THE LOVE I LOST

The Love I lost; I must go after her. The Love I Lost;
Where do I start at?
The Love I Lost; My childish ways cost me this.
The Love I Lost; If only I was given another chance with
her.
Chance can you help me find her?
The Love I Lost, know you understand.
But, is it too late, for the love I let slip away?
I'll do what ever it takes.
I'll even wait.
How long must I wait for the love that I lost?
I can remember it clearest day.
I was hight to death.
So when I came back down to life.
It was in life that I found you love.
But in death, I was the only one left.
The Love I Lost; I'll search for you until I take my last
breath.

QUESTIONS UNANSWERED

Sitting here locked off on this island with so many
questions unanswered.

Was it the fact that the ones I was directing my questions
to, didn't have the answers?

My questions were simple, or at least that I thought.

Or was it the fact that I didn't know how to ask the
questions to get the answers in the first place?

It could've been both.

And, even if I would've gotten the answers to my
questions, how would I have handled it?

And did I really want the answers to the questions I was
asking?

Or was I afraid of the circumstances that would have been
brought about from those answers?

Why am I ready for them now?

Did it have anything to do with me being locked off on this
island, and I forgot to mention, with all these books, to
really think about, there's a lot of questions unanswered?

Is my, reading these books, formulating the questions in
the first?

And finding out that the life I was living was something that I didn't have a hand in?

Then who's hands was it?

Did my loved ones know anything about this?

And if they did know, how long and why didn't they let me know?

If I can't get these questions answered, should I go to God?

Damn! I can't do that!

I was told, "Boy, don't you question God. Do as you're told".

That really left a lot of questions unanswered.

I can't even question the Creator.

And He has the manual to the whole thing; to all my questions and these hidden jewels in my dreams.

I don't know.....I just continue to have questions unanswered.

A FEELING LET GO

Scared to look passion in it's eyes.

Boggled down by the drought of love.

Once was connected like, skin and bones.

But dis-eased, from wanting that happy home.

A feeling that needs to be let go.

Will drowning in sorrow, from the pain I've caused you in your life, be swept over by, "I'm sorry?"

How many times do I need to call and tell you that, what I've did in the past, is now in the past?

I drove by your feelings, and it looked right pass me.

Where was it going? It definitely wasn't going in the direction I was headed.

My friends keep telling me to let go.

But go where? To someone else's arms, kisses and hugs?

A empty home, which was once filled with, joy and love.

The type of joy and love that any man dreams of being a part of.

But, the night mare on Elms St. delivers the death blow of defeat.

In the beginning, full of heavenly passions; now, in the end, hell is pulling drastically.

Disconnecting the umbilical cord that connected our feelings for each other; with the cord being left attached to me.

Now long days and hard nights, got my mind taking flights,
about the plights of the situation.
A deep sleep engulfs my mind with the flood of hope; in
seeing my way out of a situation that I got myself into.
A voice say, "Wake up man! Why is you drowning in
yourself in sorrow?
The same thing I put in her, I put in you."
Woke, invigorated with the destiny of meeting Destiny.
Passing by looking straight ahead at Love.
A stronger force than feeling.
Willing to go over board in the sea of forgetfulness, not
forgiveness, forgetfulness.
My asking for forgiveness has run out with what you've
given me, but your back to see.
I would say, go ahead, there's no love lost.
But I'll definitely be lying.
But I can say, life goes on, on to the next poem.
A feeling let go by time to heal and to grow and to show
that at some point any person's life, you must let go of
your half when the second have pulls away.

Made in the USA
Middletown, DE
20 March 2023

27169780R00024